# STORY MAPS

## Wayfinding Tools for the Modern Seeker

# STORY MAPS

## Wayfinding Tools for the Modern Seeker

by Michael Kass

illustrations by Julia Albain

Story & Spirit

Published by Story & Spirit
2019

Copyright © 2019 by Michael Kass

All rights reserved. This book or any portion thereof may not be reproduced or used in any manner whatsoever without the express written permission of the publisher except for the use of brief quotations in a book review or scholarly journal.

First Printing: 2019

ISBN: 9781090333001


Story & Spirit
207 N. Avenue 55, #5
Los Angeles, CA 90042

www.storyandspirit.org

# Contents

Acknowledgements ................................................................ 8
Foreword ............................................................................... 9
Exploring the Book ............................................................. 12

**Part I: Connecting with a Sense of Purpose**
Introduction ........................................................................ 16
The First Agreement of the Soul ....................................... 18
The Word and The Crosswise Word ................................. 21
And Sky Woman Fell .......................................................... 24

**Part II: Wayfinding in the Dark**
Introduction ........................................................................ 30
The Medicine Spiral ........................................................... 41
Bring the Man to Me .......................................................... 45
The Felt Sense .................................................................... 49

**Part III: Staying on the Path**
Introduction ........................................................................ 56
Nature Walks ...................................................................... 57
Animal Cards ...................................................................... 59
Breathing ............................................................................ 61

**Part IV: The Big Picture**
Introduction ........................................................................ 65
No Iceberg Floats Alone .................................................... 66
The Three Cultures ............................................................ 72
Tikkun Olam: Repairing the World .................................. 76

**Final Thoughts** .................................................................. 78
**Resources** .......................................................................... 80
**About the Author** ............................................................. 81

# Acknowledgements

This book and the expansive journeys and adventures that preceded it would not have been possible with a host of teachers, mentors, friends, and guides (both seen and unseen) that have lent support along the way. These tools are offered with tremendous gratitude to Diego Palma and Milagros, Angela, Mike Bodkin and Renee Sweezey, Diana Wyenn, Mark Risher, David Elliott, Deena Metzger, Michael Brian Baker, Barb Groth, Jeff Nixa, Dawn Revett and Christopher Frederick, Sara Isaacson, the miraculous Julia Albain, the Big Mystery, and the folks I've had a chance to work with and support over the last few years. You are all my teachers and I sure am lucky to have you.

# Foreword

When I was 9 years old, my fourth grade class took an 'urban orienteering trip' to downtown Washington, D.C.. We split into groups of 5 and set off from Alexandria, Virginia with the mission of navigating our way to the National Zoo, then to a restaurant for lunch, then back to school.

This was long before the days of smart phones, so each group had a map, a compass, and a subway map.

And an adult. We also had an adult.

As we made our way through the city, we would stop every so often and consult one of our tools. The subway map helped us negotiate transfer points. The street map helped us get from the subway to the zoo. Once at the zoo, we used internal signs to get us from the polar bears to the monkey house.

The compass wasn't useful at all, but it felt cool to have it swinging around my neck.

Later that year, the class took a trip to the mountains of West Virginia where we had another, very different, opportunity to practice orienteering skills. This time, our teachers tasked us with getting to the top of a fire break without following a set trail. Again, they gave us tools:

A compass.
A topographical map.
A pencil and ruler.
An adult.

This time, the tool that had been useless in the city became indispensable. We would walk a hundred yards or so and stop. The person holding the compass would hold it still, orient us, and we would consult the map to make sure we were heading in roughly the right direction. We repeated this process again and again, correcting course when necessary, until we made it to the top.

Ten years ago, long after those orienteering journeys, I unwittingly placed my foot on a path of personal and spiritual growth.
At the time, I had no idea what was going on.

I only knew that I felt heavy, constricted, angry, disappointed, and frustrated with myself for feeling all of these things in spite of living a life that was, by all external accounts, blessed and privileged beyond belief.

Intact nuclear family, check.
Fantastic private school education, check.
Opportunities to travel, check.
Friends and community, check.
Gainful employment with an organization that Made a Difference, check.

All the pieces were in place.

So why did I feel like such a ball of failure, unworthiness, and seething resentment?

Why did I feel so lost?

Today, I would call the feelings I experienced ten years ago symptoms of 'soul sickness,' an existential crisis brought on by the soul's desire to express its purpose in the world. At the time, I had none of that language or understanding. I didn't carry that story. All I knew was that my therapist had diagnosed me with 'dysthymia,' long-term low-grade depression punctuated by more severe episodes that worsen over time. I knew that she wanted me to try medication. And I knew that something in me knew that wasn't the right path.

I did not know what the 'right path' looked like, where it headed, or why I should take it.

And that sucked. It was terrifying.

My first bumbling steps were driven by a desire to feel less awful.

I tried meditation and even found myself in a healing breathwork class where everyone smelled like patchouli and gazed at each other with disturbingly soulful stares.

I went to Israel in search of my spiritual heritage and instead ended up finding a deep sense of not-belonging. And delicious falafel.
Without navigational tools, I set off in multiple directions, sometimes all at the same time.

In many ways, the past ten years have been about following different paths, experimenting, following my ever-sharpening intuition and internal compass to experiences, communities, rituals, and relationships that have expanded my map of what's possible.

The journey has involved rites of passage including working with plant medicines, traditional wilderness quests, walking on fire, and reading hundreds of books. It's been beautiful, rigorous, shattering, hilarious, and filled with unexpected twists at every surprising turn. Along the way, I've assembled a toolkit of navigational aides.

This book represents an effort to distill some of that into a few useful pages.

Here you'll find maps, instruments, measuring tools, and metaphorical magnifying glasses to help you along the often winding, looping, and all around confounding path of personal and spiritual movement. The toolkit is by no means comprehensive and you may find some of the tools not particularly useful. But, like the compass in the city, you may find them cool to have. Just in case.

The navigational aides in this book come from a rich field of traditions, systems, and approaches. You'll find divination techniques, breathing exercises, myths, poems, and cosmological frameworks. You will not, however, find a comprehensive, holistic 'system' or detailed road map to Spiritual Enlightenment. You get to develop that on your own.

My goal is to provide you with options, windows, ideas, and techniques to help you stay oriented on your path, wherever on that path you may be.

# Exploring the Book

When you open a tool box and dump it out, some tools are immediately recognizable and useable—a screwdriver—and some may require a bit of explanation. The maps and tools in this book are no different.

Some, such as the Nature Walk, are simple and straightforward. Some of the more involved stories ask for context and pathways to give you a way in. I've tried to provide framing and guidance when appropriate. Whatever I've provided is far from comprehensive. Please feel free to make these stories and tools your own. And if you come up with something cool, let me know!

The book itself is organized into four parts. The first revolves around connecting with a sense of purpose, the second introduces stories and tools to help reorient and find your way when all seems lost, the third offers quick techniques that can give a helpful nudge at a fork in the road, and the fourth is on establishing the Big Picture, larger frameworks that can hold all of this seeking and work.

You can read it straight through, flip to a random page, or check out the table of contents and see what feels interesting. It might be fun, for example, to read this book back to front.

Finally, a word on the title of this book. **Story Maps: Wayfinding Tools for the Modern Seeker.**

**Story** is more than a communication tactic or form of entertainment. It is the basic building block of communication and one of the most powerful creative and collaborative tools that we have. The stories we carry about the world, ourselves, and ourselves in the world create the lens that filters and inevitably distorts our perception. The path of the **modern seeker** is the path of learning to let go of stories that may have been thrust upon us by circumstance and building the capacity to craft new stories in collaboration with the world around us.

As we build this capacity, we create a new map for our world, charting out new landscapes that allow us to move differently, often with greater purpose and connection.

The path is fraught with challenges, tricky bits, and dead ends. That's where the wayfinding comes in. This 'seeking' process has been around at least as long as we have and there are literally millions of wayfinding tools left behind by those who have come before us. The modern world has largely forgotten these tools, relegating them to the disdained dustbins of 'new age mysticism.' In that process, we've cast aside a ton of wisdom.

The next 80 pages contain 14 tools, some straight from the source and some adapted, each of which can open the door to a whole realm of exploration and inquiry. If you find that a particular tool resonates strongly, check out the Resources section at the end of the book for a list of sources divided by section.

My deepest hope for this book is that you find it as interesting and useful to read as I found it to be in the writing.

Happy Trails!

# Part I: Connecting With A Sense of Purpose

# Introduction

Every journey begins with a purpose. We are either moving *away* from something or *towards* something.

When I unwittingly started the journey that lead to writing this sentence, I knew only that I deeply needed to get away from the feelings of inadequacy, resentment, and crushing insecurity that had been weighing on me for my entire life. There was no sense of having a 'purpose,' 'finding my bliss' (whatever that means), or being of service in the world.

The cultural narratives and myths that I had grown up with were dominated by stories of underdogs overcoming incredible odds to Win and Become Heroes. Rocky coming from obscurity to battle Apollo Creed. Lloyd Dobbler winning the love of Diane Court in *Say Anything*. The peasant boy Luke Skywalker discovering that he is part of an intergalactic legacy of sorcerer, ninja, laser wielding space protectors (or Jedi, if you prefer).

I loved those stories.

Part of me identified deeply with these prototypical heroes. I wanted to take the Hero's Journey and emerge victorious!

Two things stood in my way.

First, my life was pretty frictionless. Unlike the heroes in these movies and even those who I saw lionized in popular culture, I had no particular challenges. I had a solid family, great education, and had the basic privilege of being born white in the Greatest Country in the World. Sure, I had my stumbling blocks–that little voice in my head telling me that I was worthless, for example–but compared to others, I had nothing to complain about.

Second, I had no grounding in myths or stories that reinforced the idea that I could possibly have any kind of innate purpose. I had always measured my value against externally imposed metrics.

Getting the best grades.
Getting into the best schools.
Getting cast in plays.
Hanging out with the popular kids.

For three decades, these sources of validation motivated me. When I hit my 30s, their luster began to wane. Without external validation, I had no guiding star and faced the seeming-truth that I had no intrinsic value.

The stories in this chapter come from across time and cultures. All of them grow from the same basic core belief: that we are each born with a purpose. That we all have a unique role to play in the ongoing co-creation of the Universe.

I've chosen these stories because I experienced each of them as a whisper through the centuries reminding me that I have purpose and that each step along the path doesn't just carry me away from the pain I grew up with, it also carries me towards something that is both useful and beautiful. I hope they speak to you, as well.

# The First Agreement of the Soul

*I honestly do not remember the first time I came across this story. It appears in all sorts of texts, from 'The Genius Myth' by Michael Meade to various science fiction and fantasy books.*

In ancient Jewish mythology, they say that all life begins at the roots of the Tree of Life. Each individual soul, nourished by the waters of life that flow around the tree, takes shape in the Tree's roots. As the soul matures, it moves up through the Tree to its branches, ripening like a fruit. When it's ready, the soul falls from the Tree into a timeless place called the *Guf,* or Treasury of Souls.

I think of this like a celestial gumball machine, souls jumbled up waiting for some Higher Presence to turn the knob that will release one into the world.

The old myth says that it's the Archangel Gabriel who reaches into the Treasury and picks a soul out to be birthed into the mortal world. Separated from the other gumballs, this soul enters the domain of the Angel of Conception, Lailah. She places the soul into the dark cave of the human womb.

Lailah means 'night,' but the angel doesn't leave the new soul in darkness. Instead, she places a candle at its head. By the light of this candle, the soul can see from one end of the world to the other. A comprehensive view of life beyond time. A preview of things to come and of things that have been.

In this moment, the soul comes to an understanding of its unique purpose in the world. It makes an agreement to come to Earth to fulfill this purpose.

When the time comes for the soul to leave the inner realm, Lailah blows out the candle. And in the moment before the soul is born into light, she places her fingers against the soul's lips, that's where the weird indent over our lips comes from. That touch erases our memory of our purpose and of the vision we've had in the womb, buries it deep inside to be rediscovered later. It all disappears with a gentle, whispered exhale.

The journey of life, in some ways, is the journey to remembering the vision and understanding we had before coming to this world. It's a journey towards remembering that first agreement and expressing the soul's purpose in the world.

**Using This Story as a Navigational Aid**
Light a candle and take a deep breath. Either focus on the flame or allow your eyes to gently close.

As you breathe, imagine yourself back in the space between worlds. Between Spirit and Birth. You are floating, with Lailah's candle providing a gentle, warm light.

Call in your angels, guardians, and guides. If you already have a relationship with them, great. If not, there's no need to know who or what they are. Calling is enough.

Surrounded by your guides, invite in a remembrance of the vision your soul had in the moments before birth. Turn your head to the left and allow yourself to see to the beginning of time. Turn to the right and see to the end of time.

If no 'visions' come to you, that's fine. It's more than enough to simply notice how your body responds to turning left and right.

Breathe deeply and feel yourself held by the light of the present moment. With each breath, you are part of an unfolding conversation between everything that has been and everything that will be. Simply by breathing, you are fulfilling your purpose.

Keep breathing without expectation. Accept anything that comes up (or doesn't come up) without judgment.

See what happens next.

Repeat.

# The Word and The Crosswise Word

*This map came to me, again, via Michael Meade who derived it from a small village along the Amazon.*

Every soul is born with an innate purpose, a **Word** that has come to be expressed in the world. This word is not necessarily a 'word' in the literal sense. It may be a dance, a piece of music, a specific way of being. Everyone's word is unique and absolutely essential to the functioning of the Universe.

Now, if we could all bounce out of bed and go about expressing our Word, our purpose, willy nilly the world would exist in a state of perfection. That's too easy, so we also all carry a **Crosswise Word** that blocks the expression of the Word. Like the Word, the Crosswise Word is unique to each individual and is uniquely suited to block the expression of the individual's purpose.

The Word and the Crosswise Word are inextricably linked and intertwined. When one moves, the other moves to counter. They exist in a state of tension.

You get a promotion at work and that little voice inside immediately tells you that you don't deserve it, that you'll be discovered as a clueless ninny.
You sit to write a book and find yourself beset with little demons that say that you have nothing worthwhile to say.
You meet someone amazing who seems to like you and start to doubt their judgment. How could someone so fantastic have any interest in you?

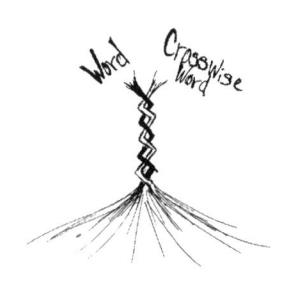

However it manifests, the tension between the Word and the

Crosswise Word tends to get more intense over time. Without intervention, they may end up in a deadlock. That deadlock can show up as anxiety, depression, irritability, inflammation, indigestion, insomnia, lack of focus, and other generally unpleasant maladies. Often, we do whatever we can to alleviate these symptoms or numb them out. For me, that looked like drinking, casual sex, and eating endless pans of brownies. This worked for a time. And then it didn't.

If the Word and Crosswise Word were the only elements at play in this map, it would essentially be a recipe for disaster. Luckily, there's a third element: **The Word Held in Waiting.**

Unlike the Word and Crosswise Word, the Word Held in Waiting doesn't exist in our day to day existence. Rather, it hangs out in an in between place, the 'Spirit' world, more closely connected with the elements, the Divine, or universal energy. Just as we each have a unique Word and Crosswise Word, we each have a unique Word Held in Waiting, almost like a guardian angel who appears when she is most needed to break the stalemate between the opposing forces inside of us.

The Word Held in Waiting may come to us in dreams or sacred ceremonies. She appears in moments of inspiration like a lightbulb popping on above our heads. The appearance of the Word Held in Waiting may be accompanied by a feeling of exhilaration or lightness, as if a great weight is falling away. Or it may be heralded by the gentle click of ancient remembrance.

When the Word Held In Waiting in in play, the tension between the Word and the Crosswise Word eases and we can perceive them as separate entities. While it may be tempting to work towards battling the Crosswise Word with the goal of obliterating it, these moments of connection facilitated by the Word Held in Waiting reveal that our soul's purpose, the Word, requires its opposite to achieve its full expression.

The Word and the Crosswise Word, in other words, each serve the deeper mission of the soul.

## Working with The Word and Crosswise Word

Some people I work with have found simply learning about this construct to be incredible helpful in creating a context for the sense that they often find themselves embroiled in inner conflict around their sense of purpose and mission in the world. Others choose to use it as an invitation for exploration. Here are a few questions to help guide that exploration:

- Where in your life do you feel the presence of the Word and Crosswise Word? How have they shown up for you?
- What are three times that you have felt the presence of The Word Held in Waiting? What has been the impact of each?
- How might you be able to create more opportunities for the Word Held in Waiting to reveal herself?

# And Sky Woman Fell

*This is a much abbreviated version of a Creation Story told by the Haundensaunee people. It came to me via Robin Wall Kimmerer in her book 'Braiding Sweetgrass' and oral retellings over the years. The full version takes many days to tell and stretches far beyond the events described in this story. This is a taste.*

Long, long ago, in the world we now inhabit, there was no land, just water and creatures of the water. But, up above, there was a place called Karonhia:ke, The Sky World. In Sky World there were beings who were in some ways like human beings and in some ways they were different. The beings in Sky World had more powers and strength than human beings have; for instance, they could make things happen just by thinking about it!

There was a tree growing in the center of Sky World called the Tree of Life. On that tree grew many different kinds of fruit and the blossoms on that tree glowed a most beautiful light that lit up Sky World. The beings in Sky World were told not to disturb that tree, but one day, a woman who was expecting a baby, asked for a drink of tea made from the roots of the Tree of Life. Her name was Atsi'tsiaka:ion which means Mature Flower.

When her husband started to dig near the bottom of the tree to get at the roots, the dirt caved in and some say that the tree fell down creating a massive hole in the floor of Sky World. This was terrible.

The woman went to see what had happened. Some say that she lost her balance while gazing, and fell into the hole. Some say that she knew she was destined to go through that hole, her insights coming from dreams she had had, and so she jumped. Some say that she was pushed. Nevertheless, when she did fall she grabbed some seeds from the roots of and around the Tree of Life. Because she fell through the hole in the sky, many people refer to her as Sky Woman.

Down below, there was a flock of water birds flying through the air. Some say they were geese. Some say they were blue heron.

Some say they were swans. One of them looked and up and saw Sky Woman falling. He spoke to the other birds and they decided to make a great blanket with their bodies and catch her on their backs. When they caught her they tried to bring her back up toward the Sky World, but she was too heavy and so they lowered her to the water below.

A giant turtle said that they could put her on his back, that his shell would be able to support her, so that's what they did. That is the reason some people call North America, Turtle Island.

Sky Woman thanked the creatures, she said that she needed land in order to survive and help other nourishment to grow. She explained Sky World to the creatures and described things that were in existence in Sky World and how she would need some of them in order to continue her life in the new world here.

The birds and turtle wanted to be of service and knew they needed help. So they called a council of all the creatures. Together, they decided to try to help Sky Woman.

One by one, the animals dove down to try to get dirt from under the water. They all dove down as far as they could (some went so far that they didn't have enough air to get back to the surface), but none were able to dive deep enough to collect dirt from the bottom of the sea.

After a time, only one animal was left: the muskrat, widely known to be the weakest diver of all the animals. As the other animals looked on doubtfully, muskrat took a deep breath and flung himself beneath the water. The animals and Sky Woman waited. And waited. Several minutes later, a small stream of bubbles broke the surface followed shortly thereafter by muskrat's lifeless body.

They all mourned muskrat and, as they did, one of the animals noticed that he had not come back empty-handed. In his paw, tightly held, was a small clump of mud.

The turtle offered to hold the mud and Sky Woman gently spread it on his shell. She sang and danced and as she did, the turtle's shell grew and the grains of dirt multiplied. As a gesture of gratitude, Sky Woman took the seeds from the roots of the Tree of Life and planted them in the brown dirt of the newly formed land. From those seeds sprouted all the colorful trees, flowers, and fruits of the earth. With so much abundance, many of the animals joined Sky Woman living on, and with, the Land.

The story goes on from here, detailing the lives and travail's of Sky Woman's children. But we will leave her here, rejoicing with the animals on the newly formed Turtle Island.

### Working with And Sky Woman Fell
Mythic stories like this burst with relevance, meaning, and metaphor. In fact, it's so ripe that, when I really focus on the tale, it starts to overwhelm me. Luckily, elements within the story itself suggest one way to work with it.

Throughout the story, certain details are left flexibly vague. No one quite knows how or why Sky Woman fell. Were the flying birds geese? Or cormorants? Doves? Who knows.

The softness of certain details invites us to take in the deeper themes and way of being at the roots of the story. Here are a few that immediately reveal themselves to me:

**The power of community and collaboration.** When they see the woman falling from the sky, the birds immediately work together to save her from certain doom. Turtle volunteers his shell and, without regard for their very important agendas, the animals gather in council to decide how best to manage the situation for the good of all involved.

**The integral role of every participant.** Every single animal that gathers has a role to play; their voice is valued as part of the conversation. Ultimately, it is the unlikely muskrat that provides the missing element to ensure the survival of Sky Woman. If any of the voices were missing, the entire council would fall apart.

**The central role of reciprocity and gratitude.** Turtle Island emerges through an exchange of gratitude, with Sky Woman offering her song, dance, and seeds from the Sky World as a gesture of appreciation for the support of the animals and for muskrat's sacrifice. This idea of exchange lies at the heart of the story.

The first time I encountered this story, I imagined what it would have been like to grow up with it as a creation myth instead of the Garden of Eden. The version of the Adam and Eve story I grew up with was fairly horrific, the couple being cast out of Eden for the sin of coveting knowledge and distrusting their God. The themes that worked their way into my psyche involved exile, division, and shame.

This simple thought experiment brought tears to my eyes as I retroactively applied it to moments from childhood and beyond. Here's one way to do this for yourself:

Imagine being a child and sitting around a campfire with other children and a storyteller. Leaning forward until their face is fully illuminated, the storyteller begins weaving the tale of Sky Woman and her fall to our realm. Imagine taking in the details: feeling the power of the birds as they flock together to soften the woman's fall. The moment that muskrat surfaces, his body floated lifelessly on the gentle sea, small paw grasping a bit of mud from the depths. Feel the vibrations of Sky Woman's dance and song as she spreads mud and seeds over the expanding shell of the generous and wise turtle.

See what happens if you imagine the story as a seed that takes root in your heart and gently spreads its influence through the estuaries of your being. You can even imagine that child sharing the same story with you in a moment of feeling lost or disconnected from a sense of purpose.

The story asks us to imagine what becomes possible if we all have an innate purpose and share it with each other courageously and with deep trust.

At least that's what it asks me.

What does it ask you?

# Part II: Wayfinding in the Dark

# Introduction

In most myths and old stories, there comes a moment when all seems lost. Snow White has bitten into the poison apple and fallen into a death-like slumber. Percival sinks in despair and gives up any hope of ever finding the Holy Grail. Having lost her slipper and returned to her humble existence, Cinderella despairs of ever seeing her prince again.

Or, in my case, a guy who seems to have everything going for him can't shake the feeling that he's living someone else's life and tumbles into a dark hole, sitting on his couch for days on end unable to move.

At these moments, connection to purpose, to the threads of our lives, falters and the path disappears. Secretly, we are still on a path, but it is hidden. We are on a pathless path.

It's an uncomfortable feeling, to say the least.

The maps and tools in this section are intended to help you get your bearings in challenging moments. I've found them particularly powerful when my stomach clenches, my jaw tightens, and the shadow of despair comes creeping into my heart. I've also found them useful on Tuesdays. Hopefully you will, as well.

# The Medicine Spiral

*This map represents a synthesis of a few different experiences and initiations I undertook between 2014 and 2017 and integrates teachings from a Wilderness Quest, storytelling experience, and over 30 years of being a confirmed movie geek. Hope you find it useful and interesting in moments of disorientation.*

Like many kids growing up in the 80s, I loved Star Wars. And Labyrinth. And Ghostbusters. And The Hobbit. And When Harry Met Sally.

As diverse as these stories were, they shared a common core: the model of growth that they hung their narrative on was linear.

In all cases, an unlikely hero became aware that they had some Greater Destiny. In order to fulfill this destiny, the hero had to overcome a set of challenges that brought them face to face with their 'shadow'; a darkness that lurked within and was made manifest in external enemies. Darth Vader. The Goblin King. The Stay Puff Marshmallow Man. Their own resistance to romantic entanglement.

By the end of the movie, the hero had emerged victorious, a stronger version of themselves. And they lived happily ever after.

With this 'Hero's Journey' hardwired into my brain, I naturally assumed that my own process of personal growth would mirror that which I had consumed throughout my childhood and adolescence. After all, what is the purpose of story if not to prepare us for the challenges of life?

Imagine my confusion and pain when I found myself confronting the same challenges over and over again. No sooner than I would emerge victorious from a battle with, for example, low self-esteem and feelings of unworthiness, than the same foe would pop up again, perhaps in a different form. Clearly I was doing something wrong. My inability to vanquish my enemies pointed to some intrinsic deficiency in my approach. Perhaps even in my soul.

Over time, and with much work to rewire narrative structures that had worn deep grooves into my brain, I learned to think about this type of work differently: it's not about victory or defeat. It's about an iterative journey.

The new narrative framework crystalized for me last year during a weeklong workshop revolving around Medicine Wheel Teachings.

The Medicine Wheel appears in cultures all over the world in a myriad of forms. In the United States, we are most familiar with it as part of Native American culture. There are hundreds of different iterations of the Wheel used by various Tribes. The people who lead the workshop I participated in confronted the spectre of cultural appropriation right off the bat, tracing the lineage of the teachings they shared from their roots through to the elder who shared the teachings with them and gave them permission to pass them on.

We focused on the Wheel as a way of understanding processes of change and transformation. In concrete terms, the Medicine Wheel consists of a circle anchored by the four cardinal directions and, in the center, the Earth below, the Sky above, and the Heart within.

Each direction corresponds to a different color, emotion, time of life, and animal. Entire books could be, and have been, written about the intricacies of Medicine Wheel teachings. If you're interested in diving more deeply into Medicine Wheel teachings, I recommend *Compass of the Heart* by Loren Cruden and *Seven Arrows* by Hyemeyohsts Storm.

For our purposes, here is an overview of the version that we worked with during the workshop to lay the foundation for the framework I'll be introducing shortly:

South:
The South is the direction of Summer and Childhood. It is characterized by strong emotions, an earthy sensuality, innocence, play, and an emphasis on basic physical survival. The color associated with the South is Red, the animal is the Mouse. When someone is caught in a whirlwind of emotions or experiencing a 'fight or flight' response, they may be 'stuck' in the South part of the Medicine Wheel.

West:
The West is the direction of Fall and Adolescence. It is characterized by introspection, fear, self-doubt, and 'shadow' elements. The color associated with the West is Black, the animals are Bear and Rattlesnake. When someone, or a community, is caught in a sense of self-reflective despair or a pattern of avoiding parts of themselves that they do not wish to acknowledge, they may be 'stuck' in the West.

North:
The North is the direction of Winter and awakened Adulthood. It is characterized by doing work in the world that is aligned with a sense of purpose and service. The color associated with the North is White, the animal is the Buffalo. While the North is the direction of integrated action, it also has a shadow side. Workaholism, an overly rigid mindset, or worked focused on function over purpose may indicate that someone is stuck in the North.

East:
The East is the direction of Spring and both Elderhood and Infancy. It is the direction of both endings and beginnings

characterized by illumination, intuition, connection with Spirit, transformation, rebirth, and creativity. The color associated with the East is yellow, the animals are the Eagle and Hawk. People or groups that indulge in 'magical thinking' and stay resolutely in the 'light' may be 'stuck' in the East.

The Medicine Wheel and the directions are powerful tools for reframing growth as a cycle and connecting the personal journey with the cycles of nature.

During the workshop, we did exercises designed to explore each direction. For the North, our task was to incorporate elements found in the desert landscape to create a picture of our Work in the world, almost like a coat of arms for our deeper purpose.

We were to find a spot in the desert and take two hours to complete the task.

The moment that I heard the assignment, a clear image appeared in my head. Not just in my head. It resonated through my body, vibrating at a soul level.

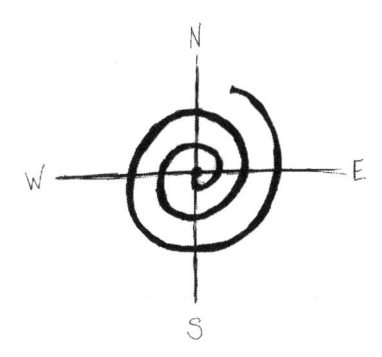

This image, a Medicine Spiral, encapsulated the way I had come to see the journey of personal growth or 'inner work,' as well as growth and change at an organizational, community, or society wide level. There are two key elements here: The spiral and the cardinal directions.

The spiral implies that growth occurs in a non-linear trajectory. While we may encounter the same challenges time and time again, our relationship to those challenges and the context around them changes with each iteration. For example:

In sixth grade, my best friend (who I also happened to have a huge crush on) padded up to me in the library and whispered into my ear that she hated me and never wanted to speak to me again. My entire body lit up with shame and self-loathing. If someone who I had trusted and, yes, loved had this reaction to me, then I must be a monster unworthy of affection or respect.

The 'shadow' in this case was a deep feeling of unworthiness triggered by a capricious rejection at the hands of a pre-adolescent girl.

Three decades later, that shadow extended over me again, this time at a New Years Eve firewalk in the mountains of New Mexico. Just before scampering over red hot coals, we were to shout out a word that held our intention for the year ahead. The rest of the group, 28 people lined up on either side of a 30 foot long bed of coals, would then hold their arms up and chant that word as we ran down the coals, literally burning the intention into our souls.

When my turn came, I called out my word: 'LOVE.'

In unison, the group started chanting 'love, love, love' over and over.

I ran down the coals.

When I reached the end, I did not feel exhilarated or loved. I felt unworthy. Something about running through a tunnel of love over fire had triggered, or enflamed, deep feelings of inadequacy. How could I be worthy of such an honor? Who was I to deserve love? I was a fraud who should be exiled.

These were the same feelings that I had experienced at the age of 12. Then, they had driven me to hide under the bleachers for three months, licking my wounds and feeling sorry for myself. Now, though the 'foe' was the same, I was different. I had new tools and a wealth of experience to draw on.

At the firewalk, I staggered to the bathroom under the weight of my self loathing, and crashed to the floor sobbing for about 10 minutes. Then I emerged and began writing, working through the sensations moving in my body. I breathed deeply. I accepted a hug. Two hours later, still shaken, I was able to rejoin the group and sing, or at least lip sync, to ring in the new year.

Since then, the shadow has appeared a few more times. Each time the feeling has been more or less the same. But my relationship to that feeling, and the tools I have to navigate it, has evolved.

In the old schema, the 'Hero's Journey' linear depiction of growth, the recurrence of the same challenge could be seen as a 'downfall' or even backsliding. The spiral model renders 'backsliding' impossible: we are always moving forward and challenges may recur when we reach the same point at a different 'ring' of the spiral.

All of this begs the question: if we are growing in a 'spiral,' what are we moving towards? What lies at the center?

This is where the second element of the model, the cardinal directions, comes in.

On its own, the 'spiral' floats in the ether; each person or situation moving in isolation, not grounded in a greater picture or cosmology. Layering the directions of the Medicine Wheel on top of the spiral provides grounding and a greater sense of 'location' within the journey.

No matter where we are in the spiral, we can pause, breathe, and locate our position both within the spiral and in relationship to the four directions.

Returning to the example above:

Examining the feelings of unworthiness, I realize that they grow out of a deep fear that I am somehow not 'enough,' a fear that if people really saw me, they would turn away in disgust or, even worse, indifference.

This fear lives in the West in the Medicine Wheel. It is a part of moving from the innocent, primal instincts of childhood in the South to the embodied, purposeful action of adulthood in the North. If I were to plot my confrontations with this fear experienced at 12 and 36 on the Medicine Spiral, it might look like this:

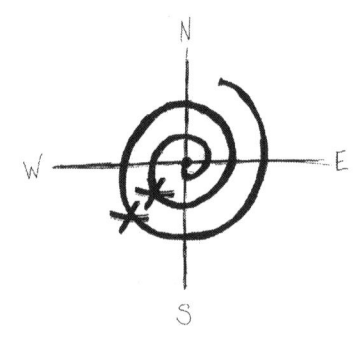

The 'x' on the outer ring is the experience at 12, the one on the inner ring is the experience at 36. While this spiral only has a few rings, I think of it as having an infinite number. But that's kind of hard to draw!

Visualizing the story this way helps in a couple of ways:

First, it allows me to see that grappling with my old friend is part of an iterative process, a journey towards aligned action and work in the world (the North) and connection with Spirit (the East) that repeats throughout life.

Second, it reminds me that with each iteration, the movement is towards center.

Center, in this structure, represents the perfect balance between all four directions. It is the place where Earth, Sky, and Heart all align perfectly. While we may stumble into a feeling approximating 'Center' from time to time through meditation or other practices, most of us truly reach center only in the moments of Birth and Death.

Earlier, I mentioned that this model works just as well as for social or communal change as it does for the growth of the individual. Let's briefly look at the recent resurgence of nationalism and white supremacy, both in the United States and around the world. There is nothing new about these movements. They flare up when a group that perceives itself as being in power experiences fear that their dominance is threatened.

Instead of thinking of these flare ups as 'cyclical,' what happens if we think of them as iterations along the medicine spiral?

The 'cycle' image implies a narrative of repetition. Each time society experiences a flare up, the response and experience will be more or less the same.

The spiral image, in contrast, presents the opportunity for learning and change. With each iteration, the fear driving those who participate in nationalist movements remains the same but the circumstances around that fear have changed. Today, for example, the internet has made immediate communication through social media possible, allowing voices that have been suppressed during previous iterations to be heard.

Furthermore, the cardinal directions allow us to reframe the current sociopolitical climate. Instead of repeating history, or even taking a step backwards, we are moving through a collective 'West' moment, defined by fear, introspection, and sometimes pain. All of which are necessary to move through as we travel towards a more aligned way of Being in the world.

As we each move through our individual journeys within a larger human journey that takes place within an all encompassing universal journey, a mindboggling image of spirals within wheels within spirals within wheels, all interlocking and impacting each other emerges.

All of which is kind of cool to think about. But how is it useful?

Our brains interpret our experience of the world by placing it within a narrative framework. When that framework is linear, or even cyclical, it can lead to feelings of defeat, frustration, and depression when we feel that we are stuck or backsliding. When confronted with a challenge we have seen before and supposedly overcome, we may interpret it as a failure or loss.

The medicine spiral provides a narrative framework that holds space for connection, ongoing growth, and repeated confrontations with blocks and challenges throughout life. It renders the idea of being 'stuck' or 'failing' meaningless. We are always moving forwards, pulled towards center by the gravity of our lives.

In my experience, it makes life feel much more like an adventure than a series of tasks or challenges to be successfully completed.

## Applying the Medicine Spiral
Here are a few ways to play with this tool:

1. Pick a place in your life where you feel challenged or 'stuck.' Plot it on the medicine spiral. What direction is it associated with? Where have you experienced this challenge before? What has changed between then and now? Where is the opportunity to move differently with this iteration?

2. Pick one direction and notice what parts of your life, past or present, resonate with it. For example, what parts of your life live primarily in the South? Where are you most playful, physical, or embodied?

3. Where do you see the medicine spiral mirrored in nature? What natural cycles and iterations can you observe each day?

4. See how the medicine spiral constructs maps to an organization or company you work or are involved with. How might it help navigate a process of organizational growth or change?

# Three Levels of Awareness

*This sketch of a map comes by way of a lecture by James Hillman and Michael Meade.*

There are three levels awareness. With practice, we can view any situation or relationship through the lens of each level.

## Factual
At this level, we are communicating and listening to ourselves and others at the level of objective 'fact.' Simple mathematics, directions, yes or no questions. The factual level holds the world of raw data, no interpretation. It is a singular level of understanding. Think of a series of unconnected points of information.

## Psychological
At the psychological level, a layer of interpretation enters the picture. This is the realm of analysis and duality, the interplay of two elements, the linear world of cause and effect. At this level, we perceive and strive to understand binary relationships. Mother / son. Husband / wife. Wife / wife. Husband / mother. You get the point.

In Western culture, we can get stuck at the psychological level, endlessly analyzing our complexes, relationships, and neuroses in a never-ending effort to gain understanding and awareness. There is nothing wrong with awareness. . . And the obsession with gaining awareness can become a proxy for actual change.

## Mythic / Poetic
The mythic level introduces a third element to the mix: the Divine, Cosmic, Soul, or, if you want to get Jungian, Collective Unconscious. This third element exists beyond the ability of the conscious mind to comprehend and is both universal and

experiential. Ecstatic poetry such as that shared by Rumi, Hafiz, Mary Oliver, David Whyte, Langston Hughes and others exists at the Mythic level, communicating deep Truths across time.

If the Factual level consists of points and the Psychological level of lines, then the Mythic level consists of three dimensional triangles, pyramids, or even overlapping spheres.

## Playing with the Levels

Take a moment to identify a place in your life where you feel confused, lost, or stuck. If that feels too intense at the moment, any place in your life where you feel particularly connected and in a state of flow works just as well.

Now we'll examine that space through the lens of each level of awareness:

## Factual

What facts do you have about this situation? No interpretation, here. Just points of data.

For example, if you feel professionally stuck and like you're wasting your life (which I certainly have), the facts might be:

I have had my current job for 4 years.
My salary has been the same for 4 years.
I feel constricted in my chest when I think about going to work.
My significant other and I fight at least twice a week.

At this level, we are simply taking an inventory of facts around the situation we have identified.

## Psychological

What relationships, past and present, have or are impacting this situation? What does that impact look like?

Continuing the example above, I might say:

My relationship with my parents, specifically in their relationship to work, feels relevant. Growing up, I saw how much they hated their jobs. And yet those same jobs provided us with a mortgage and food. So the message I received was that work that is financially supportive must also be miserable. And I am living out that story.

And so on.

At this level, we are bringing an element of storytelling and relationship into the picture.

### Mythological

Since this level introduces a third element to the scenario, it makes sense to look outside of yourself for help accessing the mythic perspective. Examples of places to look include poetry, nature, meditation, breath work or any practice that invites in elements of Spirit, cosmic, or greater intelligence.

Continuing the example above, I might seek out a poem such as *Bring The Man To Me* (also included in this section). Reading the poem, I feel a sense of kinship with the main character and his situation, along with the beautiful language that the poet uses, gives me perspective and comfort.

Alternatively, I may find a quiet place in nature and sit for awhile, observing the world around me and seeing what messages it may hold. Trees, for example, are great teachers, their roots growing deeply into the darkness of the soil in order to support growth. From the perspective of a tree, my current dis-ease could be a precursor to a period of expansion.

The possibilities are endless.

With practice, we can gain fluency in these three different layers and perspectives, learning to zoom in, out, and around various situations and relationships. The idea is not necessary to find **the right answer**, but rather to become acquainted with deeper stories and frames that can introduce previously invisible possibilities. In those moments where all seems lost and we feel hopelessly stuck, the possibility of possibility can be more than enough.

# Bring the Man to Me

*This poem comes from the collection 'The Gift,' poems by Hafiz as interpreted by Daniel Ladinsky.*

A Perfect One was traveling through the desert.
He was stretched out around the fire one night
And said to one of his close ones,

"There is a slave loose not far from us.
He escaped today from a cruel master.
His hands are still bound behind his back,
His feet are also shackled.

I can see him right now praying for God's help.
Go to him.
Ride to that distant hill;
And about a hundred feet up and to the right
You will find a small cave.
He is there.

Do not say a single word to him.
Bring the man to me.
God requests that I personally untie his body
And press my lips to his wounds."

The disciple mounts his horse and within two hours
Arrives at the small mountain cave.

The slave sees him coming, the slave looks frightened.
The disciple, on orders not to speak,
Gestures toward the sky, pantomiming:

God saw you in prayer,
Please come with me,
A great Teacher has used his heart's divine eye
To know your whereabouts.

The slave cannot believe this story,
And begins to shout at the man and tries to run
But trips from his bindings.
The disciple becomes forced to subdue him.

Think of this picture as they now travel:
The million candles in the sky are lit and singing.
Every particle of existence is a dancing altar
That some mysterious force worships.

The earth is a church floor whereupon
In the middle of a glorious night
Walks a slave, weeping, tied to a rope behind a horse,
With a speechless rider
Taking him toward the unknown.

Several times with all of his might the slave
Tries to break free,
Feeling he is being returned to captivity.
The rider stops, dismounts – brings his eyes
Near the prisoner's eyes.

A deep kindness there communicates an unbelievable hope.
The rider motions – soon, soon you will be free.
Tears roll down from the rider's cheeks
In happiness for this man.

Anger, all this fighting and tormenting want,
Sweetheart,
God has seen you and sent a close one.

Sweetheart,
God has seen your heart in prayer
And sent Hafiz.

### Exploring the Landscape of the Poem

For most of my life, I found poetry to be intensely annoying. Reading the work of Wordsworth, Shelley, Rumi and others, I found myself rolling my eyes. 'Why don't they just say what they *mean?*' I asked. It took years before I realized that they *were* saying exactly what they meant. It's just that conventional language did not have the capacity to hold what they wanted to communicate.

Since that moment of realization, I've fallen in love with encountering poems like *Bring the Man To Me*.

Here are a few questions to play with after reading the poem:

- What character do you resonate with the most? What about their situation resonates most with you?
- What images stick with you? What do they stir up within you?
- Hafiz often refers to himself as a Friend and his poems as a balm for suffering or weary souls. What comfort does this poem offer? What message does the poet have for you at this moment?

The first time that I came across this poem, I identified heavily with the slave. I had left a nonprofit career that had sustained me for nearly two decades, essentially dumping my life out on the ground to sort out the pieces. While I knew that the career and other elements hadn't been the right 'fit,' that they had been a 'cruel master,' I was terrified that I would go broke, lose my apartment, and perhaps become a crack addict.

This terror, like the slave's in the story, wasn't entirely rational. Like the slave, I felt like I was being dragged, kicking and screaming, towards an uncertain future. Also like the slave, I had become blind to the beauty all around me. The poem crossed my path at the perfect moment to remind me to look up and take in the metaphorical stars. It felt as if Hafiz had reached across the centuries to lend comfort in a challenging moment.

Years later, I picked up a book of poetry and happened to flip to this poem again. By now, I had been doing healing work with people for a couple of years. This time, while I still identified a bit with the slave who escapes only to stumble over his shackles, I felt a stronger connection with the man sent to guide the slave. The man's plight, trying to communicate with his terrified charge, reminded me that sometimes my job was not to explain, but rather to offer gentle, silent guidance, allowing my clients to become aware of, and eventually free themselves from, their own shackles.

That's me. How about you?

# The Felt Sense

*The tools we have played with so far work primarily with the mind and imagination. This approach to working with resistance or disconnection, adapted from the groundbreaking work of psychologist Eugene Gendlin as set forth in the book 'Focusing', works somatically to unlock the deep intelligence, wisdom, and intuition that we carry in our bodies.*

When encountering resistance, most of us (or perhaps just me) approach with a sense of frustration, anger, or fear.

We're **angry** because this resistance *keeps getting in the way!*
We're **frustrated** because we had a breakthrough in therapy or otherwise dealt with this resistance and yet *it's still here!*
We're **fearful** because we've come to identify so much with our resistance that we're *afraid of what might happen if it leaves.*

All three of these approaches work to keep the resistance in place or even make it stronger.

**The first step in working with resistance is getting to know it.** As we become familiar with the various ways 'resistance' shows up in our lives, we can start to craft a new relationship with it.

Please take your time with this. The questions are simple *and* working in this way can, perhaps ironically, stir up some resistance. If that does happen for you, that's totally fine. You can notice it, take a deep breath, and decide when it feels right to continue.

If you get to the point that it doesn't feel right to continue, that's fine, as well.

**Preparation**
Before you start, take a minute or two to connect with a place in

your body that feels strong, vital, and in a state of openness or flow. Follow your intuition on this; there's no right way to do it.

Once you've connected with this place (it may be as small as your right pinky!), hang out with it for a bit. Thank it for its strength. You can get really curious about the energy in this place: what color is it? What shape? Does it have anything to share with you?

If you start to feel at all overwhelmed or overly uncomfortable during the exercise, invite yourself to return your attention to this place of strength, wholeness, and well-being. Use this place as a resource throughout this exercise.

**Step 1: Connecting with Resistance**
Take a moment to ask yourself how your life is going right now. How are you in this moment? What may be holding you back from stepping forward in whatever area you'd like to make progress?

As answers come to you, you don't have to go *into* them with the goal of conscious understanding. The goal is to maintain a bit of space between you and the answer, allowing the body to respond. Where in your body do you feel and hold these answers? Where does resistance live in your body?

**Step 2: Spend some time with your Resistance**
Again, without seeking to dissect, analyze, or understand, spend some time observing this *felt sense* of resistance. If it gets too intense, you can always go back to your 're-source' space identified during the preparation.

As you spend time with your resistance, see what happens if you get curious about it.

What color is it?

What shape and consistency?
What temperature?
What texture is it?

Make note of any answers that come to you. If nothing comes to you, that's totally fine. You can take a break or reframe the question like this: 'If something *were* to come to me in response to the questions above, what would it be?'

**Step 3: Finding a Handle or Name**
Now that you have more information about this felt sense in your body, what is its quality? See if a name or word comes to you. It might be a word like *tired, judgement, jumpy, heavy* or it might be an image or phrase.

Once something comes to you, test it against the felt sense. Does it feel like the right fit? If not, allow a different handle to come to you and test it again. Repeat until you have a handle that feels right.

As you work with the sense in this way, you may find that it starts to shift or move. That's fine; just stick with it!

**Step 4: Ask the Felt Sense (or whatever name it would like) how long it has been in your body.**
Again, no right answers here. We're creating space for the answers to come in!

Write down the answer.

**Step 5: Engage in Dialogue with the Felt Sense**
*Begin the dialogue by asking this energy what it said it would do for you when it took form in your body.*

Again, allow space for the answer to come in. If it helps, you can take a rock or other object and imagine that you are putting the spirit of this energy into it. Then you can talk to the rock. It's fun!

Write down the answer and notice anything that may be starting to shift or move for you. It's not uncommon to feel emotions begin to flow at this point.

Remember, you can always take a moment to shift your attention back to the place of strength you identified earlier to re-source yourself.

*Continue by asking the energy what it needs to feel more whole, healed, and safe.*
Allow the answer to surface in its own time. It may come as words, images, or simply a felt sense in the body. As you work with this resistance energy, invite yourself to observe the sensations without labeling or interpreting them.

For example: We often experience tightness in the chest and immediately label it as 'stress', 'fear', or some other emotional experience. See what happens if you allow yourself to simply see it as 'tightness in the chest', then allow **it** to let you know what it needs and represents.

*Finally, ask this energy what small, unburdensome step you can take to make it feel more whole, healed and safe.*
The actions that come out of this step may feel unrelated to the place you're feeling resistance. For example, if you've been feeling lower back pain and stuck in your creativity, the Resistance Energy may tell you it needs you to drink more water.

The underlying idea here is that everything in our lives–internal resistance, external resistance, stress, relationships, etc.–is connected and that our body and the 'energies' within it carry deep knowledge and wisdom that we don't give ourselves the chance to access that often.

The body carries an inherent understanding of interconnection. So if it tells us that standing on one foot and singing the lyrics to *Hamilton* will help resistance in the lower back clear... it's worth a shot. Plus, singing *Hamilton* is always a good idea!

**Step 6: Check in and notice anything that has shifted**
Often, engaging in friendly dialogue with parts of ourselves that have been feeling constricted can help shift the felt sense. Take a few deep breaths and notice anything that may have shifted during this process.

You can even go back to the initial questions, how am I in this moment, and see if the answer is any different.

**A Note:**
This exercise takes us relatively quickly into a place of partnership and co-creation with areas of resistance or disconnection in our body and, because it's all connected, our lives.

It's common, especially if you're new to this type of work, to feel a sense of overwhelm, resistance, annoyance, etc. with this process. It's fine to only do a couple of the questions if that feels right. Bringing even a little more awareness to the body and to our areas of resistance is a significant step.

# Part III: Staying on the Path

# Introduction

From time to time, we all need a bit of reassurance. We're generally sure that we're heading in the right direction, but perhaps the light has gotten a bit dim and we're slightly disoriented or disconnected. I've found the tools in this section to be helpful in reconnecting with intuition and guidance.

Like this introduction, they are brief, to the point, and designed to have immediate impact.

# Nature Walks

This simple, beautiful practice is ideal for moments when we feel slightly disconnected or in need of light guidance. We're reasonably confident that, generally speaking, we're on the right rack, but perhaps the path has gotten a bit muddy.

Before setting out, spend a few minutes feeling into a question or intention. The more simple the question, the more specific the response will be. For example, 'What should I do with my life' might be a little complex for this exercise. 'Should I take this job' or 'how should I handle x' are a bit more specific.

With this question in your heart, find a place in nature and, before stepping too deeply into it, stand at the threshold. Breathe deeply and send a prayer to the trees and creatures around you. Express gratitude for their presence and ask for their guidance.

The moment you take a step from the threshold, everything you see, hear, and experience is a response to your question. As you walk, allow your senses to heighten and become more acute. Notice how each external stimulus provokes an internal reaction. How does the sound of a bird singing affect you? What was in your mind at the moment the wind rustled through the leaves above?

With each step, imagine the earth rising up to support your weight. Find a tree that feels interesting and touch its bark. See if it has a message for you.

Walk, wander, and adventure until you feel an internal shift around your question. When you feel complete, make sure to leave something for the forest, or beach or wherever, in exchange for the guidance you may have received. This can be a small crystal, flower, tobacco, leaf of sage gathered with permission. Something natural.

## A Walk in the Park

A few months ago, I was feeling disconnected and out of sorts. Not in a major 'my life is ending way,' more in a 'mild funk' way.

Lacing up my hiking shoes, I drove 20 minutes to a forested area near me in Los Angeles. Before I started my walk, I set an intention: Please help me get reconnected so I can be of service. Then I started walking.

Within a minute, a beautiful hawk swooped past me and alighted on a branch no more than 20 feet away. It gazed at me, unblinking. I gazed back and felt my chest begin to loosen. I had gotten so wrapped up in the day to day tasks of survival and 'work,' that I had lost the big picture. The hawk reminded me to create space for the broader perspective, the literal bird's eye view.

No sooner had I come to this realization than the hawk bobbed its head and set off in search of prey.

As the walk continued, I felt energy returning to my body. The trees waving gently in the light breeze reminded me that deep roots and foundation support sustainable growth and resilience to winds. A dragonfly reminded of the beauty all around me lurking in the smallest detailsWith each step, I became more and more aware of the vast interconnected web of life humming around me. Before leaving the trees, I poured a little water on the parched earth in gratitude.

By the time I returned to my car, just half an hour later, I felt rejuvenated, open, centered, and embodied.

Sometimes it really is that simple.

# Animal Cards

Over the past three years, I've developed a fun practice using Animal Spirit cards. I use the deck produced by *The Wild Unknown*, but any deck would work just as well.

Each animal in the deck represents a different archetypal energy and carries a different message. In the *Wild Unknown* deck, the Turtle, for example, is an ancient soul, embodying grounding, deep trust, and belonging to the self. When in balance Turtle energy is peaceful, adventurous, and productive. When out of balance, the Turtle slows to a halt. To bring the Turtle back into balance, the Wild Unknown recommends taking an adventure. Fun!

Here's one way to use these, or other, cards when feeling a bit stuck or out of sorts:

Take a moment to center and ground. I'll sometimes light a candle or bit of sage and take a few breaths.

When you feel present, allow a question or request to enter your mind. As you hold the question, begin shuffling the deck in whatever way feels right to you. As you shuffle, a card may jump from the deck. If it does, that's your card. If not, you can ruffle through the cards until you find the one that wants to play. It may have a slight vibration or simply feel, in some indefinable way, 'right.'

Once you have selected your card, sit with it for a moment before finding the guide book's description. Take in the art. Where does your eye go first? What elements pop out? Does anything on the card feel particularly attractive? Or dissonant? What energy or message does this animal seem to embody?

As you spend time with your animal, notice how your body responds. Even before delving into the 'meaning' of the card, what messages might it hold for you?

When it feels right, find your card in the deck's guidebook and read the description. Here are a few questions to play with:

- How does the description resonate with what you intuited before reading the guide?
- How could this animal's energy be a response to your question or request?
- What about your question or request could have attracted the energy of this card?
- Does this animal's energy feel in balance or out of balance within you?

Working with these questions and anything else that may come up, journal or sketch for a few minutes, then see what may have shifted over the course of your brief encounter with this animal spirit.

The idea with these cards is less that they are predictive, oracle like emanations from the Spirit Realm (though they may be), but rather that they provide a way of becoming more present with your inner world so you can tap into your intuition and inner guidance system.

For what it's worth, I've also found that working with the animal cards as opposed to other decks, like Tarot, helps me move through my day with a greater sense of connection to the natural world.

# Breathing

Sometimes slight feelings of disconnection, anxiety, or disorientation can be assuaged through simple conscious breathing.

Have you ever noticed what happens to your breathing when you're stressed or experiencing high anxiety? If you're like most people, it becomes constricted or even stops altogether. You may feel a tightness in your chest and your shoulders creep up to somewhere around your ears. Your body's 'fight, flight, or freeze' instinct activates and your higher cognitive functions are slightly depressed. It's no fun.

We've evolved to have this response. Back in the day, when we were hunter / gatherers living in the wild, the stress response was pretty useful. It allowed our brain to divert resources to things that would ensure our survival, like running quickly away from tigers. When we escaped the tiger, the stress response would dissipate.

We no longer live in that world. Today's world seems designed to provoke a near-constant state of stress and anxiety.

There are emails to return, the TV is on, telling us how awful the world is, we have to return that call about that thing, the health insurance billing got screwed up and WHY did my car insurance overcharge me AGAIN?! and. . . hang on, I'm getting a text, have to answer it immediately because what if he/she is the ONE, lol. . . You get the point.

Our brains are overwhelmed to the point that we can't breathe. Not all the time. But more than we probably think.

But never fear! We actually have the built in ability to reduce the stress response through conscious breathing. Here are three quick exercises that you can do anywhere, anytime that you become aware that your breath has gotten away from you.

## The Big Sigh

This one is so easy it's almost funny. Step 1: Take a nice, deep inhale through the nose. This should be relaxed and full--imagine your diaphragm and torso filling with air like a balloon. Step 2: Exhale with a big, audible sigh. An exaggerated sigh. A luxurious sigh that lets the world know that you are enjoying the hell out of that sigh. If you really want to get into it, say the words 'Calgon Take Me Away!' as you sigh. Or not. That part is optional.

Repeat at least 5 times. It should take a minute or less. Notice what happens in your body as you do the exercise!

## The Box Breath

This is another simple, powerful exercise you can do anywhere. Inhale through the nose on a four count. Hold it for a four count. Exhale on a four count. Hold for four. Then do it again. For this one, you can alter the count if four seems too long or short. The objective is to breathe in a controlled, conscious way for at least 5 repetitions.

Next time stress or anxiety take your breath away, use one of these exercises to take it back. The key is to bring awareness, to become really conscious of and present to the breath. We can always choose to reclaim the brain--all it takes is a deep, conscious breath.

## Three Connected Breaths

I use this simple three breath sequence to bring myself back into connection with myself and the broader world any time I start to feel unmoored. It's also great for grounding a group before meetings or to close a group. Here's how it works.

*Take a deep breath.*

With this breath, we connect with the self. This is the foundation of most breath-based practices: bringing awareness to the feeling of the breath entering and leaving the body. Connecting with the breath, and the energy it brings to the cells helps us reestablish a link with ourselves and the processes that happen in the background in each moment to keep us moving.

As you breathe in, imagine the oxygen flooding into the cells. As it penetrates through the cellular membrane, it fuels the mitochondria, allowing the cells to power up and do their work.

As you breathe out, imagine all the spent energy leaving the body as you prepare for an infusion of new, fresh energy with the next inhale.

You can go as far as you'd like with this visualization. Imagine energy, carried by the breath, as a current running through your veins and capillaries, washing away indifference and bringing fresh energy to every cell, organ, and muscle in the body.

*Take a second deep breath.*

With this second breath, we connect with the world around us. As you breathe, bring awareness to the fact that the molecules of air entering your body might have been inside someone else less than 10 minutes ago. A day ago, they may have been inside a giraffe in Africa, a political leader, or a prisoner half a world away. Each breath is quite literally a point of connection with every plant and animal in the known world. Imagine where the particles moving through your body may have been moments ago, a week ago, a year ago and allow yourself to perceive yourself as part of a vast web of connection and exchange.

*Take a third breath.*

The third breath connects us across time. Because matter can neither be created nor destroyed, the molecules we breathe have been around in one form or another since the beginning of time itself. And they will be around, in some form, until the end of time.

As you breathe, imagine yourself participating in a process that extends from one end of time to the other. With each breath, you are part of a vast interconnected web of inhales, exhales, and exchange. You are at once a miniscule part of the web and utterly indispensable to its function. Without your breath, the system doesn't work quite right.

Whenever your world starts to feel a little flat, dull, or routine, try taking a few deep breaths and invoking these three dimensions of connection. Connecting deeply with the breath even once a day can help foster greater presence and invite a sense of the sacred into your life. If we can bring a sense of mystery, wildness, and surprise to the breath, imagine what is possible in even the most 'domesticated' corners of life.

# Part IV: The Big Picture

# Introduction

When I first started going to therapy in my 30s, I was dogged by the suspicion that it was all incredibly privileged and self-indulgent. That suspicion was exacerbated by the fact that I had no larger framework or cosmology within which to place the work I did in my therapist's office. I was simply miserable and wanted to be less miserable.

Given that people in my city were literally dying on the streets, that felt pretty petty.

As I've connected with stories and systems that encourage a wider, more holistic view of inner work, my beliefs have shifted. The models and stories in this section present frameworks that I hope will answer questions like 'how can I take time for this when people are in very real suffering all around me?' Or 'what is the point of all of this? Just to feel better?' Or 'How does connecting with my purpose make a dent in the world's ills?'

They've certainly helped me grapple with those questions. Perhaps you'll find them powerful, as well.

# No Iceberg Floats Alone

I first came across the 'iceberg' as a metaphor during a session with my therapist over ten years ago. I had been grappling with the idea that the way I experienced myself was not at all how the world experienced me.

She nodded and drew a simple image on her pad:

Icebergs, she told me, are much larger than they appear. Only 10 to 20 percent of an iceberg is visible above the water. The rest lurks below, under the surface. The same is true of people. We only see what's on the surface, people's behavior and their actions in the world. There's so much more beneath the surface, a whole world of emotions, thoughts, and feelings. What you're describing, she told me, is a disconnect between the top and bottom of the iceberg.

The metaphor blew my mind and stuck with me.

A few months ago, I found myself meditating on the power of ritual and prayer. The iceberg came floating into my mind, but instead of focusing on the iceberg itself, my attention focused on the water around it. An expanded version of the metaphor emerged that resonated so strongly that I popped out of my meditation and scrawled it on a scrap of paper. Here's what I drew:

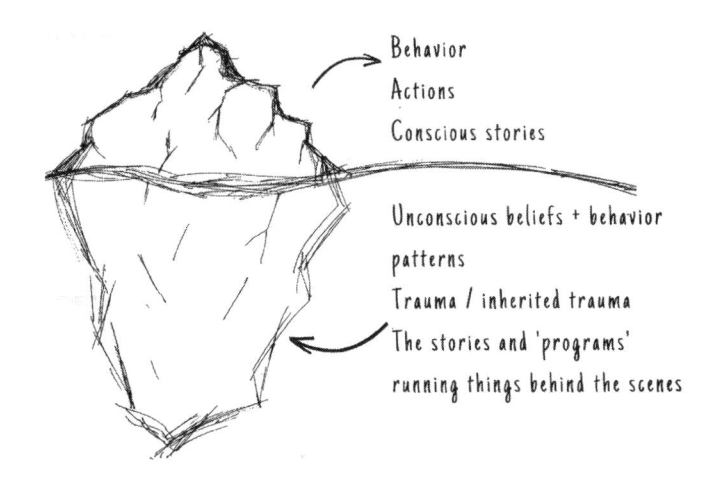

*Above the waterline:*
- Behavior
- Actions
- Conscious stories

*Below the waterline:*
- Unconscious beliefs + behavior patterns
- Trauma / inherited trauma
- The stories and 'programs' running things behind the scenes

On the surface, we have the 10 percent of the iceberg that is visible. That's the individual's behavior, actions, and the stories they consciously put out into the world.

Beneath the surface, we find the 90 percent of the individual that is invisible to the casual bystander. Unconscious beliefs and behavior patterns. All of those stories about ourselves and the world that we absorbed from our families, education, friends, and the world around us. This is also the level at which we might find trauma and inherited trauma, those elements of our personality that lurk in the shadows, pulling the strings and driving decisions.

Most therapy and coaching limits itself to working with these two levels of the individual, looking at how the unconscious affects the conscious and, sometimes, vice versa.

Icebergs, however, do not exist in a vacuum. They float in the ocean. As humans, so do we.

And just as the ocean supports different ecosystems at different depths, so does the 'ocean' around us.

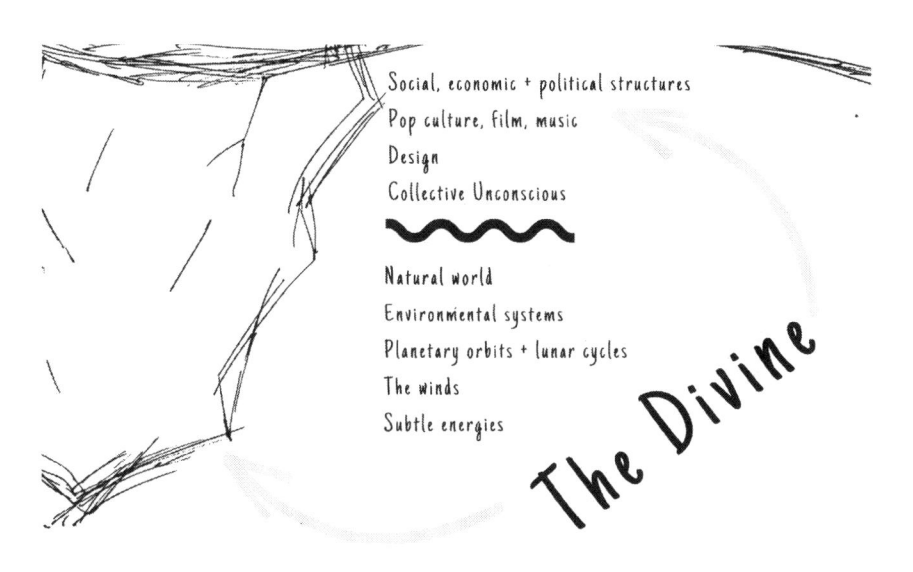

```
Social, economic + political structures
Pop culture, film, music
Design
Collective Unconscious

~~~~~

Natural world
Environmental systems
Planetary orbits + lunar cycles
The winds
Subtle energies
                              The Divine
```

At the level closest to the individual, we find the immediate environment of economic, social, and political structures. We also see pop culture, music, film, and community mythologies as well as architecture and design. All of these elements influence the collective unconscious as well as the individual's conscious and unconscious behavior.

The elements in the water closest to the iceberg stretch across different disciplines and areas, but all have one thing in common: they are all human-made.

As we move deeper into the ocean, we find the natural world, encompassing environmental systems, planetary orbits, lunar cycles, the winds, and the world of subtle energies. While our actions may influence these elements, as with climate change, they existed long before humans arrived on the scene and will exist long after we're gone.

Finally, at the deepest level, we find the Divine, Cosmic Consciousness, Universe, God or whatever term for the original creative energy you prefer.

Following the metaphor, ice both melts into the ocean and absorbs elements from the water around it. The temperature of the water influences the iceberg and the presence of the iceberg influences, even if in tiny ways, the ocean. Ice is literally made of the same basic material as the ocean around it in the same way that we, as humans, are made of the same basic energies and elements as the world around us.

It all flows together. In this system, the 'Divine' is simply the deepest, most essential element that holds the entire system together.

In this way of seeing, when we pray, engage in ritual, or conduct a ceremony, the intention, at least in part, is to appeal to the Divine. In doing so, we appeal to the common energy that flows through all living beings and tacitly acknowledge the connections that exist in the spaces between us.

Going back to my first encounter with this metaphor, I wonder what would have happened had my therapist placed the iceberg within a larger ocean. Honestly, I probably would have been overwhelmed and had a brain glitch. Since then, however, I've played with this idea both with my own inner exploration and with clients and have found that feeling into the larger context and systems within which we operate is incredibly helpful.

It reminds us that, no matter what our mind tells us, we're never truly isolated or alone.

It challenges us to recognize how our smallest actions may send ripples through the entire system. And to see how shifts in the larger system, including moon cycles and environmental shifts, may be impacting our beliefs and behavior.

It allows us to see ourselves within a larger container that can hold multiple points of view that, when viewed from the limited, individual perspective, may seem to be misaligned or in conflict.

Ultimately, we are both infinitesimally small and utterly indispensable to the vast ocean around us.

### A few questions to explore. . .
The pitfall of frameworks like this is that they appeal to the mind and may not get fully integrated. Here are a few questions and exercises to guide deeper exploration:

- Sweep your arm vigorously through the air. Now pause and imagine that your arm is shifting energy as it moves along its path. Each small shift causes a ripple effect that extends outwards. Close your eyes and sweep your arm more slowly this time, allowing yourself to feel the molecules of air shifting around you. How far does the ripple effect extend? If it feels fun, write a story about it.

- How does this 'Iceberg Model' resonate with conversations around diversity, inclusion, white supremacy, feminism, and other hot button topics?

- Looking at the whole system, what is a possible relationship between climate change and the increasing incidence of anxiety and depression in Western culture? This isn't necessarily a cause and effect relationship; we're just playing with seeing it all as an interrelated system.

- What impact might you shifting a small behavior have on your direct relationships? What impact might shifting that small behavior have on the broader environment?

# The Three Cultures

*This simple, elegant model came to me via Christina Baldwin's work and book 'Calling the Circle.' It also resonates with many Native American, Andean, Mayan, and other indigenous beliefs and prophecies that hold that humanity has reached a pivotal moment. We can continue down the road we have walked for the past few hundred years and follow it to its natural endpoint, the end of humanity as we know it. Or we can choose a different path, integrating ancient ways of being into the modern world, finding our way back to right relationship with the Earth, and beginning a new chapter.*

*This map lays out a path for that integration.*

**First Culture**
The earliest humans needed each other to survive. Without community, they would fall victim to any number of predators. And if they managed to evade tigers and such, the elements would do them in. So early humans learned how to work together in tribes.

These ancient cultures revolved around the simple structure of the circle. Tribes would gather in circles around a fire, build circular dwellings, and hold meetings sitting in council circles. Aboriginal and indigenous art from all over the world going back thousands upon thousands of years features sacred spirals painted on cave walls and ancient pottery.

A deep sense of connection and inclusion is embedded in the idea of a circle. When we sit in circle, we belong. No one member is elevated above any other. Leadership is shared and we look each other in the eyes. The structure itself invites deep collaboration.

In old ways of thinking, the Circle did not just include humans, but also animals, plants, the stars, and the Earth. All beings were related in a vast network of interrelated circles. This shows up all over the world in the Medicine Wheel, Wheel of Life, and Wheel of the Year among others. Thousands of years before the 'wheel' was invented as a concrete tool, it existed in the collective psyche as a metaphor for a way of relating that allowed us to survive and thrive.

## Second Culture

If the circle is the symbol of First Culture, then the triangle represents Second Culture. Where the energy of the circle invites fluidity, inclusion, and equity, the triangle brings linear structure, hierarchy, and concrete definition. While there is nothing inherently wrong with these elements, they can become destructive in excess.

Over the past several hundred years, if not longer, humanity has embraced the triangle as its organizing principle. The impact has been a sense of disconnection from the world around us, from ourselves, and from each other. We are out of harmony with the planet. At the same time, many of us in the 'developed' world struggle in toxic work environments mired in patriarchal power dynamics where the greater percentage of our humanity is not welcomed.

In his book *Decolonizing Wealth*, Edgar Villanueva traces these symptoms to a root cause embedded in the project of colonization. The process of decolonization, he argues, involves shifting from division to connection. From interpersonal dynamics based on control to more relational dynamics. And from exploitation being the basis of power to belonging.

In this map, 'decolonization' is a necessary precursor to the emergence of a Third Culture.

## Third Culture

According to Christina Baldwin, a Third Culture will integrate the energy and power of the circle with the linearity and direction of the triangle. It's worth noting that the key distinction between First and Second Culture isn't that the 'circle' ever completely vanished. It's just that it has been relegated to the sidelines.

Circles still hold sway at spiritual gatherings. And campfires. And maypole dances.

When it comes to Board Meetings, Parliamentary gatherings, and other mechanisms of power and governance, hierarchy holds the power and the triangle reigns, both metaphorically and literally. The speaker stands at a lectern, elevated above an audience that is arrayed in regiment-like rows.

Because it does not exist yet, no one is quite sure what the Third Culture will look or feel like. Baldwin posits that it will be less a fixed way of being and more a relational practice. "It is," she says, "the practice of learning how to behave with respect towards each other, toward our earthly resources, and toward Spirit. When we change how we interpret and interact with the circumstances and people around us, we create Third Culture."

In other words, if you're reading this, chances are that you're actively engaged in co-creating the Third Culture.

# Tikkun Olam: Repairing the World

*Since we started with a story from Jewish mysticism, it feels appropriate to end with another construct from the same tradition. This is severely oversimplified version of an immensely complex system. I am choosing to focus on the part that talks about the role of each individual soul in bringing healing to the world.*

In modern times, the Hebrew term *tikkun olam,* translated as 'world repair,' has become synonymous with social justice, repairing the torn fabric of our society. On a more mythic level, however, it has its roots in an ancient Kaballistic creation myth.

According to this myth, the creation of the universe was not an emanation *from* the divine, but rather a contraction of it. God, in other words, made herself smaller to make room for creation. In the process of this contraction, Divine light became contained in special vessels, called *kelim,* some of which shattered and scattered throughout the realms of creation. While most of the light returned to the Divine source, some of it attached itself to the shards. These shards constitute 'evil' and lay at the foundation of the material world; the trapped sparks of Divine light lend them power.

The old stories say that Adam's original mission was to restore the Divine sparks through mystical rituals and exercises. Unfortunately, his sin interrupted the process and good and evil remained mixed in the created world. Human souls, initially all contained within Adam's, also became imprisoned within the shards.

Each individual is responsible for helping repair the world by connecting with and gathering Divine light from their soul, separating it from the material world, and returning it to its Source. Mystical acts, ritual, and practices drive this process of universal healing. Ultimately, all the scattered light will return to the Divine and, with perfection restored, creation will cease to exist.

Within this framework, each act of meditation, conscious breath, self-exploration, and 'personal growth' no matter how small becomes part of an eons long collective mission to repair the universe.

No pressure.

# Final Thoughts

It feels a bit odd to write 'final thoughts' for a book designed to provide support along a journey that, at least on this plane, never ends. That said, this is the end of the book and I find myself hugely curious as to how you took it in.

Did you read it all in one sitting? Did it sit on a shelf for years before you picked up while cleaning? Did you read a bit of it, set it aside, and end up using it to mop up a spill? Did you find it interesting and useful?

Whatever the case, I'm hugely grateful for the opportunity to write this for you. As I've put the pieces together, new relationships between these stories, maps, and tools have revealed themselves to me.

The slave in *Bring the Man to Me* is in the process of remembering the vision that appeared to him under the care of the angel Lailah. Tuning in to the Felt Sense seems to be a powerful way to connect with the many layers of connection revealed in the Iceberg Model. And so on.

There are infinite numbers of pathways, stories, and tools and each of us is tasked with finding our own way, our own unique path through the wilds of life. One of the great lies of modern, Western myth and culture is that we must stumble along the path alone. Nothing could be further from the truth. So my final thought is an invitation:

If something in this book resonates, you have questions, something to share, or simply seek support, please feel free to reach out to me or drop by for a workshop. My contact information and schedule of events is at www.storyandspirit.org.

Thank you so much for reading and you're pretty awesome.

With Much Warmth,
Michael

# Resources

**Part I: Connecting with a Sense of Purpose**
*The Genius Myth* by Michael Meade
*Braiding Sweetgrass* by Robin Wall Kimmerer
*The Living Myth* podcast

**Part II: Wayfinding in the Dark**
*Compass of the Heart* by Loren Cruden
*The Lost Art of Heart Navigation* by Jeff Nixa
*Focusing* by Eugene Gendlin
*The Gift* by Hafiz, interpreted by Daniel Ladinsky
*The Rag and Bone Shop of the Heart*, edited by Robert Bly, James Hillman, and Michael Meade
*To Bless the Space Between Us*, by John O'Donohue
*Eternal Echoes* by John O'Donohue

**Part III: Staying on the Path**
*The Wild Unknown Animal Spirit Deck* by Kim Kranz
*Just Breathe* by Dan Brule
*To Be Soul, Do Soul* by Hiro Boga

**Part IV: The Big Picture**
*Calling the Circle* by Cristina Baldwin
*Neither Wolf Nor Dog* by Kent Newborn
*Decolonizing Wealth* by Edgar Villanueva
*American Indian Prophecies: Conversations with Chasing Deer* by Kurt Kaltreider, Ph.D.

# About the Author

**Michael Kass** is the founder of *Story & Spirit* and is passionate about helping people, organizations and communities discover and harness the power of their stories to create change. That passion has somehow led him to working with everyone from CEOs in Istanbul to inmates in California's Central Valley. His workshops and trainings on storytelling, speaking, mindfulness and breathwork have been featured at events around the world.

Also a performer, Michael's storytelling has appeared on podcasts including *I Love a Good Story, Taboo Tales,* and *Story Worthy*. His solo show, *Ceremony: A True Tale of Love, Fear, and Ayahuasca,* toured nationally and garnered awards including LA Weekly Pick of the Week, and best of Fringe awards in Los Angeles, San Francisco, San Diego, and Chicago.

Michael is an ICF Certified Coach, Breathwork Facilitator, healer, human and probably likes brownies more than you do.

Learn more at www.storyandspirit.org

Made in the USA
Middletown, DE
23 March 2019